UNCONVENTIONAL MONEY-MAKING METHODS: EXPLORING UNIQUE PATHS TO FINANCIAL SUCCESS

TABLE OF CONTENTS

Introduction: Redefining Success: Beyond the Conventional Notions of Wealth

Part I: Unconventional Side Hustles

- The Rise of the Side Gig Economy: Embracing Opportunities in the Gig Economy
- From Passion to Profit: Turning Your Hobbies into Income-Generating Ventures
- Making Money from Your Skills: Freelancing and Consulting in the Digital Age
- The Art of Thrifting: Flipping and Reselling for Fun and Profit
- Unique Service-Based Businesses: Unleashing Your Creativity and Problem-Solving Skills

Part II: Creative Online Ventures

- The Digital Content Revolution: Monetizing Your Online Presence

- YouTube, Twitch, and Beyond: Earning from Online Video Content

- Podcasting for Profit: Tapping into the World of Audio Entertainment

- Niche Blogging: Building Authority and Generating Income through Blogging

- The Power of E-commerce: Launching and Scaling a Successful Online Store

Part III: Investing Outside the Box

- Beyond Stocks and Bonds: Alternative Investments for Diversification

- The World of Cryptocurrencies: Opportunities and Risks in Digital Assets

- Impact Investing: Making Money with a Social and Environmental Conscience

- Arts and Culture Entrepreneurship: Navigating the Business of Creativity
- Non-Profit and Social Entrepreneurship: Creating Impact and Income
- Innovative Funding Models: Crowdfunding and Beyond

Conclusion

Embracing Unconventional Paths: Building a Sustainable and Fulfilling Financial Future

Appendix

Resources and Tools: A Comprehensive Guide for Aspiring Unconventional Entrepreneurs

INTRODUCTION

In a world that often equates success with material possessions and financial abundance, it's time to challenge the conventional notions of wealth and redefine what it means to be successful. This book, "Unconventional Money-Making Methods: Exploring Unique Paths to Financial Success," aims to take readers on a journey of exploration, breaking free from the traditional approach to making money and embracing alternative and creative avenues for financial growth.

The pursuit of money and financial security is a fundamental aspect of human existence. We all strive to meet our needs, support our families, and achieve our dreams. However, the prevailing societal mindset tends to limit our understanding of how wealth can be generated and what it truly means to achieve financial success. The traditional path often dictates that we must follow a linear trajectory: go to school, get a stable job, climb the corporate ladder, invest in stocks, and save for retirement. While this approach may work for some, it's not the only path available, nor is it the most fulfilling for everyone.

This book is not about dismissing the traditional methods of making money, as they have proven effective for many individuals. Instead, it aims to shed light on the multitude of other possibilities that exist, often hidden in the shadows of convention. We will explore unconventional side hustles, creative online ventures, alternative investments, remote work opportunities, and the pursuit of passion projects as viable and exciting means to financial success.

At its core, this book is about empowerment - empowering readers to think beyond the boundaries set by societal norms, to dream big, and to discover their unique path to financial prosperity. It encourages readers to embrace their creativity, passions, and talents, and leverage them to create income streams that align with their values and aspirations.

Throughout these pages, you will encounter inspiring stories of individuals who dared to venture off the beaten path and achieved remarkable success. These stories will demonstrate that there is no one-size-fits-all approach to making money. Each person's journey is distinct, shaped by their skills, interests, and circumstances.

We will delve into the realm of unconventional side hustles, where people have found ingenious ways to monetize their hobbies, skills, and interests. From turning a love for vintage fashion into a thriving online store to transforming a passion for writing into a freelance career, these individuals have discovered that passion can indeed be a currency.

In the digital age, opportunities abound online. We will explore how content creators, from YouTubers to podcasters, have harnessed the power of the internet to build engaged audiences and generate income while pursuing their passions. Additionally, we will examine the world of remote work, where the concept of the traditional office is evolving, opening doors for location-independent careers and adventurous digital nomad lifestyles.

Investing, too, can take unconventional forms. We will venture beyond the realm of stocks and bonds to explore alternative investment opportunities that offer diversification and unique risk-reward profiles. The rise of impact investing will highlight how financial growth can align with positive social and environmental change.

This book also acknowledges the power of pursuing passion projects and creative entrepreneurship. Arts and culture entrepreneurs, driven by their love for artistic expression, have successfully built sustainable businesses around their creative works. Non-profit organizations and social entrepreneurs have shown that doing good can go hand in hand with financial sustainability.

As readers embark on this exploration of unconventional money-making methods, it's essential to approach this journey with an open mind and a willingness to challenge preconceived notions. While some paths may resonate more strongly with certain individuals, others might find inspiration in unexpected places.

The goal is not to discard the traditional methods entirely but rather to consider a broader spectrum of possibilities. By embracing creativity, adaptability, and a willingness to take calculated risks, readers can uncover paths to financial success that align with their passions and values.

So, let us venture forth into the realm of unconventional money-making, where innovation, passion, and purpose converge to create a new vision of success. Together, we will discover the boundless potential that lies beyond the ordinary, and unlock a world of opportunities on our journey towards financial prosperity and personal fulfillment. Let the exploration begin!

PART I: UNCONVENTIONAL SIDE HUSTLES

The Rise of the Side Gig Economy: Embracing Opportunities in the Gig Economy

In recent years, a seismic shift has occurred in the global job market, giving rise to what is now commonly known as the gig economy. Traditional employment models, where individuals commit to long-term, full-time positions with a single employer, are no longer the only viable option for making a living. Instead, a new era has emerged, one that embraces flexibility, autonomy, and the potential for multiple income streams - the side gig economy.

Understanding the Gig Economy: Defying Traditional Employment Norms

The gig economy is characterized by a labor market composed of short-term contracts, freelance work, and project-based engagements. Individuals, often referred to as "gig workers" or "independent contractors," work on a project-by-project basis rather than holding down a permanent position with a single employer. This dynamic allows them the freedom to choose when, where, and how much they work, creating a sense of autonomy that is highly appealing to many.

In the conventional job market, the employer typically sets the terms of employment, including fixed work hours, benefits packages, and a predetermined salary. However, in the gig economy, gig workers have more control over their work arrangements. They can select projects that align with their skills and interests, negotiate their compensation, and decide how much time they dedicate to their gigs.

The Appeal of Side Gigs: Supplementing Income and Pursuing Passions

The side gig economy is a subset of the broader gig economy, focusing on individuals who maintain a primary source of income from traditional employment while actively engaging in secondary income-generating activities on the side. Side gigs are often pursued during evenings, weekends, or spare time, making them ideal for those seeking to supplement their earnings without committing to a full career change.

One of the primary appeals of side gigs is the opportunity to pursue passions and interests that may not be feasible within a traditional job role. For example, a software developer with a passion for photography can work on freelance photography projects during weekends, enabling them to indulge in their creative pursuits without sacrificing their primary career path.

Moreover, side gigs offer a safety net during times of economic uncertainty. In an ever-changing job market, individuals recognize the importance of diversifying their income streams to protect themselves against unexpected job losses or economic downturns.

The Advantages of Embracing Side Gigs: Flexibility and Skill Development

Embracing side gigs comes with numerous advantages that appeal to a wide range of individuals. First and foremost, the flexibility of working on a project-by-project basis allows gig workers to strike a balance between their personal lives and work commitments. Parents can spend more time with their children, students can juggle their studies with part-time gigs, and professionals can explore entrepreneurial ambitions without giving up their primary job security.

Additionally, side gigs provide an avenue for continuous skill development. As gig workers take on diverse projects, they have the opportunity to expand their skill sets, gain valuable experience across various industries, and build a robust portfolio that enhances their marketability.

Challenges and Considerations: Addressing the Gig Economy's Pitfalls

While the gig economy offers a myriad of benefits, it also comes with challenges that must be navigated wisely. Gig workers often lack the benefits and protections that come with traditional employment, such as health insurance, retirement plans, and paid leave. It is crucial for individuals engaged in side gigs to carefully manage their finances, plan for tax liabilities, and explore options for obtaining personal insurance coverage.

Furthermore, gig workers need to be proactive in managing their workload and income stability. Irregular and unpredictable income can be a source of stress, necessitating financial planning and budgeting to ensure a steady flow of funds during lean periods.

Embracing the Side Gig Economy's Potential

The rise of the side gig economy represents a transformational shift in how people approach work and income generation. Embracing opportunities in the gig economy allows individuals to take charge of their careers, pursue their passions, and create multiple streams of income.

As we venture deeper into the gig economy landscape in this book, we will explore various unconventional side hustles and creative online ventures that present exciting opportunities for financial growth and personal fulfillment. With the right mindset, adaptability, and a willingness to embrace change, readers can unlock the full potential of the side gig economy and embark on a rewarding journey towards financial prosperity and professional fulfillment.

From Passion to Profit: Turning Your Hobbies into Income-Generating Ventures

The concept of turning one's hobbies into profitable ventures is a testament to the idea that the pursuit of passion and financial success need not be mutually exclusive. In the modern world, where the gig economy and online connectivity have opened new avenues for self-expression and entrepreneurship, individuals are discovering that their hobbies can be transformed into income-generating opportunities that not only fulfill their creative desires but also contribute to their financial well-being.

The Power of Passion: Unleashing Creative Potential

Passions are the driving force behind human innovation and creativity. They represent areas of deep interest, personal joy, and unique skills that set individuals apart. Whether it's painting, cooking, writing, crafting, or playing a musical instrument, hobbies often bring a sense of fulfillment that is hard to replicate in other aspects of life. They allow individuals to escape the monotony of routine, engage in meaningful self-expression, and create something that resonates with their inner selves.

By harnessing the power of passion, individuals can infuse their work with authenticity and enthusiasm, which often translates into a product or service that stands out in the market. Turning a hobby into an income-generating venture allows individuals to monetize their skills and share their creative output with a wider audience, creating a win-win scenario where personal satisfaction intersects with financial gain.

Validating Your Hobby-Based Business Idea: From Passion Project to Profitable Venture

While the idea of turning a hobby into a business is exciting, it's essential to approach this transition strategically. Validating your hobby-based business idea involves careful consideration of market demand, target audience, and revenue potential. A hobby that is deeply fulfilling to you might not necessarily align with a profitable niche, so conducting thorough market research is crucial.

Identify your target audience and assess whether there is a demand for your hobby-related products or services. Consider the uniqueness of your offering, potential competitors, and the value you can bring to your customers. By approaching your hobby with an entrepreneurial mindset, you can refine your concept to ensure it has the potential to generate income while still maintaining the essence of what makes it enjoyable to you.

Leveraging Online Platforms and Social Media: Reaching a Global Audience

The advent of the internet and social media has revolutionized the way individuals can share their hobbies with the world. Online platforms provide accessible and cost-effective avenues for promoting and selling hobby-related products and services. From e-commerce websites to social media marketplaces, these platforms enable you to showcase your creativity and connect with a global audience.

Utilizing social media effectively can help you build a brand, engage with potential customers, and create a loyal following. Visual platforms like Instagram, Pinterest, and TikTok are particularly powerful for showcasing visually appealing hobbies such as art, photography, and crafting. By leveraging the reach of these platforms, you can attract customers who share your passion and are eager to support your creative journey.

Balancing Passion and Business: Maintaining Authenticity

As you embark on the journey of turning your hobby into an income-generating venture, it's crucial to strike a balance between your creative passion and the practicalities of running a business. While passion is the foundation, effective business practices are essential for long-term success. This includes setting clear goals, creating a business plan, managing finances, and establishing efficient processes.

At the same time, maintaining the authenticity and joy of your hobby is paramount. Strive to infuse your products or services with the same enthusiasm that initially drew you to your hobby. Authenticity resonates with customers and sets you apart from more commercialized competitors.

Overcoming Challenges: Transforming Obstacles into Opportunities

Transitioning from a hobbyist to a business owner can present challenges, and it's important to approach them as opportunities for growth. Challenges may include scaling your production, managing time effectively, navigating legal and regulatory requirements, and maintaining a consistent income. Each challenge provides a chance to refine your skills, expand your knowledge, and develop a deeper understanding of your industry.

Where Passion and Profit Converge

In the modern landscape of creative entrepreneurship, turning your hobbies into income-generating ventures is a testament to the boundless potential of human ingenuity. By aligning your passions with strategic business practices, you can create a fulfilling and financially rewarding journey. From artisans selling handmade crafts to bloggers sharing their expertise, the intersection of passion and profit offers a remarkable path to personal fulfillment and success. As you embark on this exciting endeavor, remember that the pursuit of passion not only enriches your life but also has the potential to inspire and positively impact others in ways you may never have imagined.

Making Money from Your Skills: Freelancing and Consulting in the Digital Age

The digital age has brought about a revolution in the way we work, paving the way for individuals to leverage their skills and expertise in unprecedented ways. Freelancing and consulting have emerged as powerful avenues for making money from one's skills, offering a flexible and dynamic approach to earning income while navigating the evolving landscape of work.

The Rise of the Freelance Economy: Redefining Work

Freelancing, once considered an alternative to traditional employment, has evolved into a thriving global industry. The freelance economy is characterized by professionals offering their services on a project-by-project basis, often to multiple clients simultaneously. This shift has been fueled by technological advancements, such as online platforms and communication tools, that enable freelancers to connect with clients around the world.

Consulting, a closely related field, involves providing expert advice and guidance in a specific domain. Consultants are hired by organizations or individuals seeking specialized knowledge to solve complex problems or achieve specific goals. Consulting engagements can range from short-term advisory roles to long-term strategic partnerships.

Freelancing: The Art of Independence and Flexibility

One of the primary attractions of freelancing is the independence it offers. Freelancers have the freedom to choose the projects they work on, set their own schedules, and define their rates. This level of autonomy allows individuals to align their work with their lifestyle and personal preferences, fostering a sense of control over their professional lives.

Freelancers can tap into a wide range of industries and niches, from writing and graphic design to web development, marketing, and beyond. As businesses increasingly seek specialized talent for short-term projects, freelancers can position themselves as experts in their field, providing tailored solutions that meet the unique needs of each client.

Consulting: Expertise in Action

Consulting takes freelancing a step further by focusing on delivering strategic insights and solutions. Consultants are valued for their expertise and experience, and they play a pivotal role in guiding organizations toward informed decisions and sustainable growth.

Successful consultants often possess a deep understanding of their industry, strong analytical skills, and the ability to communicate complex concepts clearly. They must be adaptable and capable of crafting tailored strategies that address the specific challenges and goals of each client.

Navigating the Digital Landscape: Online Platforms and Networking

The digital age has created an interconnected global marketplace for freelancers and consultants. Online platforms like Upwork, Freelancer, and LinkedIn have democratized access to clients and projects, enabling professionals to showcase their skills, connect with potential clients, and secure work opportunities from the comfort of their homes.

Effective networking is also paramount in freelancing and consulting. Building a strong online presence, engaging with industry communities, and nurturing relationships with clients and fellow professionals can lead to a steady stream of referrals and collaborations.

Managing the Business Side: Pricing, Contracts, and Client Relationships

While freelancing and consulting offer the allure of flexibility and creative freedom, they also require diligent business management. Determining pricing structures that reflect the value of your skills, creating clear contracts, and managing client expectations are essential components of a successful freelancing or consulting career.

Establishing strong client relationships is equally important. Effective communication, understanding client needs, and delivering high-quality work on time contribute to building a reputation that attracts repeat business and referrals.

The Path to Mastery: Continuous Learning and Skill Development

In the ever-evolving digital landscape, freelancers and consultants must remain adaptable and committed to continuous learning. Staying updated with industry trends, acquiring new skills, and refining existing ones are critical to maintaining a competitive edge.

Platforms offering online courses and certifications, such as Coursera, Udemy, and LinkedIn Learning, have made skill development more accessible than ever. By investing in self-improvement, freelancers and consultants can expand their service offerings and position themselves as leaders in their chosen fields.

The Empowerment of Freelancing and Consulting

Freelancing and consulting represent a paradigm shift in the way we approach work and income generation. The digital age has empowered individuals to leverage their skills, knowledge, and expertise to create meaningful and financially rewarding careers.

The allure of independence, the potential for unlimited growth, and the ability to make a direct impact on clients and organizations make freelancing and consulting compelling options for those seeking a dynamic and fulfilling professional journey.

As the digital age continues to reshape the landscape of work, embracing freelancing and consulting offers an exciting and transformative path to financial success, personal fulfillment, and professional excellence. With determination, strategic thinking, and a commitment to continuous improvement, individuals can embark on a journey of empowerment, leveraging their skills to navigate the complex and exciting terrain of the digital age.

The Art of Thrifting: Flipping and Reselling for Fun and Profit

In a world driven by consumerism and mass production, the art of thrifting has emerged as a creative and sustainable way to shop, as well as a lucrative avenue for enterprising individuals to generate income. Thrifting goes beyond mere bargain hunting; it involves the thrill of discovery, the preservation of history, and the potential for transforming found treasures into profitable ventures through the process of flipping and reselling.

Thrifting Unveiled: A Journey of Exploration and Discovery

Thrifting is the art of scouring thrift stores, consignment shops, flea markets, garage sales, and online marketplaces in search of unique and valuable items. The thrill lies in uncovering hidden gems that others might overlook, from vintage clothing and antique furniture to collectibles, books, and electronics. Thrifting is more than just a shopping technique; it's a creative pursuit that celebrates the joy of discovery and the satisfaction of finding items with stories to tell.

Thrifting enthusiasts develop a keen eye for recognizing potential value in overlooked items. This skill involves a combination of knowledge about different categories of goods, an understanding of market trends, and a bit of intuition. What may appear as an ordinary item to most could hold significant value to collectors or enthusiasts.

Flipping: Turning Finds into Profitable Ventures

Flipping is the art of purchasing items at a lower price and then reselling them at a higher price, often after making improvements or modifications. Thrifted finds can be transformed through creative refurbishing, repairing, cleaning, or repurposing, adding value to the items before they are resold.

Flipping involves a mix of creativity, entrepreneurship, and strategic thinking. Successful flippers carefully evaluate the potential resale value of items, consider the costs of refurbishing or improving them, and factor in market demand to determine their pricing strategy.

The Thrifting Mindset: A Blend of Passion and Business Acumen

Thrifting and flipping require a unique mindset that blends a passion for treasure hunting with shrewd business acumen. On one hand, thrifting is a hobby that brings joy through exploration, nostalgia, and the thrill of discovery. On the other hand, flipping is a business endeavor that requires careful planning, financial management, and marketing skills.

Thrifting enthusiasts often find immense satisfaction in saving items from being discarded or forgotten. By breathing new life into these items, flippers contribute to a more sustainable and eco-conscious way of consuming. In a world grappling with environmental concerns and fast fashion, the art of thrifting and flipping offers a counter-narrative that champions conscious consumption and responsible stewardship of resources.

Online Platforms: Expanding the Reach of Thrifting and Flipping

The digital age has revolutionized the world of thrifting and flipping, making it easier than ever to connect with potential buyers and expand market reach. Online marketplaces like eBay, Etsy, Poshmark, and Facebook Marketplace provide platforms for flippers to showcase their refurbished or thrifted finds to a global audience.

These platforms not only enable flippers to reach a broader market but also facilitate communication with potential buyers, secure transactions, and build a reputation as a reliable seller. Additionally, social media platforms like Instagram and TikTok allow flippers to document their thrifting journeys, share their transformations, and engage with a community of like-minded individuals.

Challenges and Rewards: The Journey of a Thrifter and Flipper

While thrifting and flipping offer exciting opportunities, they are not without challenges. Flippers need to navigate factors such as sourcing consistent inventory, managing refurbishing costs, staying up-to-date with market trends, and maintaining high-quality customer service. Additionally, the competitive nature of the online marketplace requires flippers to differentiate themselves and establish a unique selling proposition.

However, the rewards of thrifting and flipping extend far beyond monetary gain. They include the satisfaction of unearthing hidden treasures, the joy of preserving history and unique craftsmanship, and the sense of accomplishment that comes from turning a neglected item into something valuable and desirable.

Where Creativity Meets Commerce

The art of thrifting and flipping is a testament to the power of creativity, resourcefulness, and entrepreneurship. It is a celebration of the potential inherent in everyday items, as well as a demonstration of how passion and business acumen can converge to create profitable and meaningful ventures.

Thrifting and flipping are not only avenues for generating income but also reflections of a changing consumer landscape that values uniqueness, sustainability, and authenticity. As thrifting enthusiasts and flippers breathe new life into discarded items and share their transformed treasures with the world, they contribute to a cultural shift that embraces the art of uncovering hidden gems and transforming them into valuable commodities. In this way, thrifting and flipping become not just practices, but a testament to the limitless possibilities that await those who are willing to see beyond the surface and reimagine the potential of the ordinary.

PART II
UNIQUE SERVICE-BASED BUSINESSES: UNLEASHING YOUR CREATIVITY AND PROBLEM-SOLVING SKILLS

INTRODUCTION

In the dynamic landscape of entrepreneurship, traditional business models are being reshaped by innovative approaches that harness creativity and problem-solving to offer unique services. Service-based businesses have emerged as a vibrant and rewarding path for individuals to showcase their talents, address specific needs, and create meaningful solutions for clients and customers.

Redefining Entrepreneurship: The Rise of Service-Based Ventures

Service-based businesses stand in contrast to product-based businesses, focusing on delivering expertise, solutions, and experiences rather than tangible goods. These businesses capitalize on the power of human skills, creativity, and knowledge to address diverse challenges across various industries.

While product-based businesses involve the creation, manufacturing, and distribution of physical items, service-based businesses emphasize the value of intangible offerings. Consultants, coaches, designers, therapists, event planners, and countless other professionals have embraced service-based entrepreneurship to showcase their talents and provide tailored solutions to clients.

The Creative Advantage: Leveraging Unique Skills

One of the defining features of service-based businesses is the emphasis on unique skills and expertise. Entrepreneurs in this space leverage their individual talents, experiences, and knowledge to offer services that cater to specific needs. These skills can range from graphic design and copywriting to life coaching, digital marketing, and beyond.

The creative advantage lies in the ability to differentiate through personalization. Service-based entrepreneurs can tailor their offerings to match the unique requirements of each client, creating a sense of value and exclusivity that is difficult to replicate with mass-produced products.

Problem-Solving as a Core Element: Meeting Client Needs

Service-based businesses thrive on their capacity to solve problems. Entrepreneurs in this realm actively listen to their clients' challenges, pain points, and goals, and then craft solutions that address these issues directly. This problem-solving approach fosters strong client relationships and positions service-based entrepreneurs as trusted advisors.

Effective problem-solving requires empathy, active communication, and a willingness to adapt. By truly understanding a client's needs and aspirations, service-based entrepreneurs can design services that not only meet expectations but exceed them, resulting in a loyal customer base and positive referrals.

Crafting Unique Experiences: The Intangible Value Proposition

In the realm of service-based businesses, the value proposition often revolves around the intangible benefits and experiences provided to clients. Consultants, for instance, offer insights and strategies that can transform a client's business. Wedding planners create unforgettable events that leave lasting memories. Wellness coaches guide individuals toward healthier lifestyles.

The art of crafting unique experiences involves going beyond transactional interactions and building emotional connections. Service-based entrepreneurs have the opportunity to create transformative moments that resonate deeply with clients and customers, leaving a lasting impact.

Navigating Challenges and Scaling Up: Balancing Quality and Growth

Service-based entrepreneurs face a distinct set of challenges, particularly as their businesses grow. Balancing quality and scalability is a common dilemma. As demand increases, maintaining the same level of personalized service can become challenging. However, scaling up can be achieved by implementing efficient processes, leveraging technology, and nurturing a team that shares the same commitment to excellence.

Additionally, marketing and branding play a crucial role in the success of service-based businesses. Communicating the unique value of your services, establishing a strong online presence, and building a reputation for reliability and expertise are essential components of attracting and retaining clients.

Shaping the Future of Entrepreneurship

In a rapidly evolving business landscape, service-based entrepreneurs are shaping the future of entrepreneurship by leveraging creativity, problem-solving skills, and personalized approaches to meet the unique needs of clients and customers. These entrepreneurs demonstrate that the true essence of entrepreneurship lies in the ability to innovate, adapt, and create meaningful impact through services that resonate with both the mind and heart.

Whether it's transforming a client's business strategy, helping individuals achieve personal growth, or curating memorable events, service-based businesses showcase the profound potential of human expertise. As individuals unleash their creativity and problem-solving skills to address specific challenges and deliver tailored solutions, they contribute to a thriving ecosystem of entrepreneurship that values ingenuity, authenticity, and the power of personal connection.

Creative Online Ventures

## 1.	Introduction to Creative Online Ventures: Navigating the Digital Frontier

In an era defined by technological advancement, the digital realm has become a vast and uncharted landscape of opportunity. Creative minds and visionary entrepreneurs are harnessing the power of the internet to embark on unprecedented journeys of innovation, transforming their passions, talents, and ideas into thriving online ventures.

Welcome to the world of Creative Online Ventures, where imagination knows no bounds, and the boundaries of traditional entrepreneurship are continually pushed. This realm is a playground of endless potential, where individuals with a unique vision can build and shape their own digital empires, reaching audiences across the globe and rewriting the rules of success.

The digital age has democratized access to the global market, enabling creators, artists, professionals, and enthusiasts to connect, collaborate, and share their creations on an unprecedented scale. From e-commerce platforms and content creation to social media influence and digital services, the avenues for creative expression and financial gain are limited only by the depths of imagination.

The Promise of Creative Online Ventures

Creative Online Ventures hold the promise of transforming passions into livelihoods, hobbies into businesses, and dreams into reality. Whether you're a budding artist, a tech-savvy innovator, an aspiring writer, or a seasoned professional looking to explore new horizons, the digital frontier offers a canvas where your ideas can flourish and your talents can shine.

In this landscape, traditional barriers to entry have been dismantled. You no longer need massive capital investments or extensive physical infrastructure to bring your ideas to fruition. All you need is a digital device, an internet connection, and the determination to carve out your space in the online world.

Navigating the Digital Frontier

While the potential for success in the digital realm is immense, navigating this frontier requires a unique set of skills, strategies, and insights. The principles of business, branding, marketing, and customer engagement take on new dimensions in the digital landscape. From mastering the art of online storytelling to leveraging social media algorithms, search engine optimization, and data analytics, there's a wealth of knowledge to be gained and strategies to be explored.

This journey is not without its challenges. The digital world is dynamic, constantly evolving, and highly competitive. Yet, with the right mindset, a willingness to adapt, and a commitment to continuous learning, the rewards are substantial. Creative Online Ventures offer the opportunity to build personal brands, reach untapped markets, and redefine success on your terms.

Embarking on Your Journey

As we delve into the realm of Creative Online Ventures, we will explore a plethora of possibilities and avenues. From launching an e-commerce store and building a strong online presence to monetizing your content and engaging with a global audience, the chapters that follow will guide you through the intricacies of this exciting and transformative landscape.

Through real-world examples, practical advice, and inspirational stories, you will uncover the tools and strategies needed to turn your creative spark into a thriving online venture. Whether you're an artist, a creator, an entrepreneur, or someone simply curious about the possibilities, this journey will empower you to take control of your destiny in the digital age.

So, with an open heart, a curious mind, and a daring spirit, let us embark on a journey through the vast expanse of Creative Online Ventures. Together, we'll navigate this digital frontier, uncover hidden treasures, and forge a path to success that is uniquely yours. The future awaits, and its time to make your mark on the world.

2.   The Digital Content Revolution: Monetizing Your Online Presence

The digital age has ushered in a revolution of connectivity, creativity, and unprecedented access to global audiences. In this brave new world, individuals and businesses alike are embracing the power of digital content to not only share their passions and expertise but also to generate income. The ability to monetize your online presence is at the heart of the digital content revolution, offering a pathway to financial independence and creative fulfillment.

Content Creation in the Digital Era: A New Frontier of Expression

Content creation has evolved from a simple pastime into a dynamic and multifaceted industry. Whether you're producing videos, writing blogs, recording podcasts, designing graphics, or curating social media posts, digital platforms have provided an outlet for virtually every form of creative expression.

This democratization of content creation is the cornerstone of the digital content revolution. Traditional gatekeepers have been bypassed, allowing individuals to share their stories, expertise, and insights directly with a global audience. The result is an explosion of diverse voices, ideas, and narratives that enrich the online landscape.

Monetizing Your Digital Presence: Transforming Passion into Profit

Monetizing your online presence involves leveraging the content you create to generate income. This can be achieved through a variety of methods that cater to your skills, audience, and goals. From bloggers earning through affiliate marketing to YouTubers profiting from ad revenue, and from podcasters offering premium content to artists selling digital downloads, the avenues are as diverse as the content itself.

The key lies in understanding your audience and crafting strategies that resonate with their needs and preferences. Monetization is not just about selling; it's about creating value for your audience while ensuring that your efforts are financially sustainable.

Building a Strong Online Brand: The Foundation of Monetization

A strong online brand is the bedrock upon which successful monetization is built. Your brand encompasses your identity, values, unique selling proposition, and the promise you make to your audience. It's what sets you apart in a sea of digital content creators and establishes your credibility.

Consistency in content quality, visual aesthetics, and messaging is paramount. Developing a brand voice that resonates and fosters engagement is equally crucial. A well-defined brand not only attracts loyal followers but also opens the door to collaborations, sponsorships, and partnerships with brands aligned with your niche.

Diversifying Revenue Streams: Beyond Ads and Sponsorships

While advertising revenue and sponsorships are commonly associated with content monetization, they are only the tip of the iceberg. The digital content landscape offers a plethora of opportunities for diversifying your revenue streams. These include:

Subscription Models: Offering premium content to subscribers who pay a recurring fee for exclusive access.

Digital Products: Creating and selling e-books, courses, presets, templates, and other digital resources tailored to your expertise.

Crowdfunding and Donations: Platforms like Patreon allow your audience to financially support your content in exchange for special perks.

Merchandising: Selling merchandise related to your brand, such as branded apparel, accessories, or even physical art prints.

Virtual Events and Workshops: Hosting webinars, virtual events, and online workshops that attendees pay to participate in.

Freelancing and Consulting: Leveraging your expertise to offer services or consulting in your niche.

Challenges and Success Factors: Navigating the Journey

Monetizing your online presence requires a combination of dedication, creativity, strategy, and adaptability. The journey comes with challenges, including algorithm changes, market saturation, and the need to consistently innovate. Staying informed about industry trends, being open to feedback, and consistently improving your craft are vital.

Authenticity and audience engagement remain central to success. An engaged community is more likely to support your monetization efforts, whether through purchasing your products, becoming subscribers, or advocating for your brand.

Empowerment in the Digital Age

The digital content revolution has unlocked a world of possibilities, enabling individuals to turn their passions and expertise into viable income streams. Monetizing your online presence is more than a financial endeavor; it's an empowerment of creativity, a celebration of individuality, and a testament to the boundless opportunities of the digital era.

As you embark on your journey to monetize your online presence, remember that your authenticity, passion, and dedication are your greatest assets. The digital content landscape is yours to shape, and with the right strategies, an engaged audience, and a commitment to excellence, you can navigate this exciting frontier and turn your creative vision into a prosperous reality.

3.   YouTube, Twitch, and Beyond: Earning from Online Video Content

YouTube, Twitch, and Beyond: Earning from Online Video Content

In the ever-evolving landscape of digital media, online video content has risen to the forefront as a dominant and highly lucrative platform for creative expression, education, and entertainment. Platforms like YouTube and Twitch have transformed ordinary individuals into global influencers, enabling them to monetize their content and build sustainable careers. In this exploration, we dive deep into the world of online video content, uncovering the strategies, challenges, and opportunities for earning from your creative endeavors.

The Rise of Online Video Platforms: A New Era of Content Consumption

YouTube and Twitch, among other platforms, have fundamentally altered how people consume content. The proliferation of smartphones, improved internet connectivity, and the appeal of visual and interactive content have fueled the popularity of online videos. Audiences are no longer passive viewers; they actively engage, share, and even contribute to content creation.

These platforms offer diverse opportunities for creators, ranging from educational tutorials and gaming streams to lifestyle vlogs and comedy sketches. Regardless of your niche, there's an audience eager to engage with your unique perspective.

YouTube: The Global Video Sharing Giant

YouTube has become synonymous with online video content. As one of the largest search engines and the second most-visited site after Google, it provides an expansive platform for creators to share their talents and insights. The platform's monetization features, such as AdSense and YouTube Premium revenue sharing, offer a pathway to income generation.

To earn from YouTube, creators can monetize their videos through ads, channel memberships, merchandise shelf integration, and Super Chat during live streams. The key to success lies in consistently delivering valuable and engaging content, building a loyal subscriber base, and optimizing videos for search visibility.

Twitch: Empowering Live Streaming and Community Engagement

Twitch has revolutionized the way people interact with content creators, particularly in the realm of gaming. It's a platform that emphasizes live streaming, real-time interaction, and fostering an engaged community. Twitch primarily monetizes through its Partner and Affiliate programs, which offer revenue sharing, subscription revenue, and bits (virtual goods).

For Twitch success, consistency in streaming, community engagement, and the creation of unique and entertaining content are paramount. Building a strong rapport with your viewers and offering them value through entertaining gameplay, tutorials, commentary, or creative content can turn your channel into a lucrative venture.

Beyond YouTube and Twitch: Exploring Alternative Platforms

While YouTube and Twitch dominate the online video landscape, they are not the only platforms where creators can thrive. Platforms like TikTok, Instagram, Facebook, and LinkedIn also offer video content opportunities. TikTok's short-form videos, Instagram's IGTV, and Facebook Live provide avenues for creators to tap into different demographics and expand their reach.

Additionally, niche-specific platforms cater to specialized audiences. For instance, Vimeo is favored by filmmakers, Skill share for educational content, and Caffeine for interactive live streaming. Exploring these platforms can help you diversify your content strategy and income streams.

Monetization Strategies and Diversification

Earning from online video content requires a multifaceted approach. While ad revenue is a significant contributor, diversifying income streams is essential for stability. This can include:

Sponsorships and Brand Collaborations: Partnering with brands relevant to your content for sponsored videos or integrations.

Affiliate Marketing: Promoting products or services and earning a commission for sales generated through your referral links.

Merchandising: Selling branded merchandise related to your content or niche.

Crowdfunding: Platforms like Patreon allow your audience to support your content through monthly subscriptions.

Digital Products: Offering exclusive content, e-books, courses, or other digital products to your audience.

The Power of Community and Engagement

Beyond monetization, the heart of online video content lies in building a community. Engagement is the key to success, as it fosters a loyal audience that actively supports your endeavors. Responding to comments, engaging on social media, and involving your viewers in your content decisions can strengthen your relationship with your audience.

Challenges and the Road Ahead

While the online video content landscape offers exciting opportunities, it's not without its challenges. The competition is fierce, algorithm changes can affect visibility, and maintaining consistent quality content can be demanding. Adapting to platform updates, staying informed about trends, and continually refining your content strategy are essential for long-term success.

Your Digital Video Journey

In the realm of online video content, creativity, authenticity, and perseverance are your guiding stars. Whether you choose YouTube, Twitch, or alternative platforms, your journey is a blend of creative expression, community building, and strategic monetization. As you navigate this dynamic landscape, remember that the power to succeed lies in your ability to connect with your audience, adapt to change, and create content that resonates and leaves a lasting impact in the digital world.

3.   Podcasting for Profit: Tapping into the World of Audio Entertainment

In the modern era of digital media, podcasting has emerged as a powerful and accessible platform for content creation, information sharing, and entertainment. What began as a niche form of communication has now evolved into a mainstream channel with a global audience hungry for engaging and insightful audio content. Podcasting offers not only a creative outlet but also a pathway to profit, enabling creators to generate income while connecting with listeners on a deeper level.

The Rise of Podcasting: A Revolution in Audio Content

Podcasting has revolutionized the way we consume information and entertainment. With the ubiquity of smartphones and the convenience of on-demand listening, podcasts have become a staple in the lives of millions. From storytelling and news analysis to self-improvement and niche interests, podcasts cater to diverse tastes and preferences.

What sets podcasting apart is its intimate and immersive nature. Listeners develop a sense of connection with hosts, often feeling like they're part of a private conversation. This personal connection makes podcasting an ideal platform for creators to share their expertise, tell stories, and engage with an audience on a deeply emotional level.

Monetizing Podcasts: From Passion to Profit

While podcasting begins as a passion project for many creators, it has evolved into a legitimate source of income. There are several strategies for monetizing podcasts, each offering unique benefits and revenue streams.

Advertising and Sponsorships: Advertising remains the most common way podcasts generate revenue. Creators can partner with sponsors relevant to their content and audience, earning income through pre-roll, mid-roll, or post-roll ads.

Listener Support and Donations: Platforms like Patreon allow listeners to support their favorite podcasts through monthly subscriptions or one-time donations, creating a loyal fan base invested in the podcast's success.

Premium Content and Subscriptions: Creators can offer exclusive or ad-free content to subscribers who pay a recurring fee, providing extra value to dedicated listeners.

Merchandising: Podcasts with a strong brand can sell merchandise such as T-shirts, mugs, or other branded items, creating an additional revenue stream and deepening listener engagement.

Live Shows and Events: Podcasters can monetize through live shows, workshops, or events where fans can meet the hosts and engage in person.

Affiliate Marketing: Promoting products or services and earning a commission for sales generated through podcast-specific referral links.

Creating Quality Content: The Foundation of Podcasting Success

Quality content is at the heart of any successful podcasting venture. To attract and retain listeners, creators must offer unique, informative, and engaging content that resonates with their target audience. A well-defined niche and clear value proposition help differentiate your podcast in a crowded market.

Effective storytelling, engaging interviews, and a conversational tone are hallmarks of successful podcasts. As you build a loyal listener base, word-of-mouth recommendations and positive reviews become catalysts for growth.

Building a Strong Brand and Audience Engagement

A strong brand identity is crucial for podcasting success. From your podcast's name and logo to your online presence and social media engagement, consistency and authenticity create a memorable and recognizable brand.

Engagement is a two-way street in podcasting. Encouraging listener interaction through calls to action, social media engagement, and listener feedback not only builds a sense of community but also offers insights into your audience's preferences and needs.

Technical and Production Considerations

While content is king, technical aspects of podcast production also play a crucial role. Quality audio, good editing, and effective use of music and sound effects enhance the listening experience. Fortunately, technology has made podcasting more accessible than ever, with a plethora of affordable tools and resources available for recording, editing, and publishing podcasts.

Challenges and Long-Term Success

The podcasting landscape is competitive, and achieving long-term success requires dedication, adaptability, and a commitment to continuous improvement. Staying informed about industry trends, refining your content strategy, and evolving with your audience's preferences are essential for maintaining relevance and growth.

Unleashing Your Voice and Creativity

Podcasting for profit is a journey that combines passion with entrepreneurship, creativity with strategy, and entertainment with education. It empowers creators to unleash their voices and connect with audiences in a deeply meaningful way while also generating income.

In an era where listeners crave authentic voices and meaningful connections, podcasting offers a unique opportunity to tap into the world of audio entertainment, leaving a lasting impact on your listeners and creating a sustainable source of income. As you embark on your podcasting journey, remember that your authenticity, creativity, and dedication are the driving forces that will propel you toward success in the exciting realm of podcasting for profit.

4. Niche Blogging: Building Authority and Generating Income through Blogging

In the vast landscape of the internet, niche blogging has emerged as a powerful and effective way to establish authority, connect with like-minded individuals, and even generate income. By focusing on a specific topic or subject area, niche bloggers can position themselves as experts, cultivate a dedicated audience, and create opportunities for monetization. In this exploration, we delve deep into the world of niche blogging, uncovering the strategies, challenges, and rewards of building authority and income through focused content creation.

Defining Niche Blogging: Going Deep in a Specific Topic

Niche blogging revolves around creating content that is tightly focused on a specific subject, theme, or industry. Unlike general or lifestyle blogging, which covers a wide range of topics, niche blogging drills down into a particular area of interest. This specialization allows bloggers to attract a highly targeted audience that shares a passion for the chosen niche.

By selecting a niche that aligns with your expertise, interests, and the needs of your target audience, you position yourself as a credible and reliable source of information. This authority is the foundation upon which niche bloggers build their online presence and income streams.

Establishing Authority: Becoming the Go-To Expert

Authority in niche blogging is synonymous with expertise and trustworthiness. To establish yourself as an authority, you must:

In-Depth Knowledge: Deepen your understanding of your chosen niche, continuously expanding your knowledge and staying current with trends and developments.

Quality Content: Consistently produce high-quality, informative, and valuable content that addresses the questions and concerns of your audience.

Original Insights: Offer unique perspectives, insights, or solutions that set you apart from competitors and demonstrate your expertise.

Engagement: Engage with your audience through comments, social media, and email, building a sense of community and fostering trust.

Collaborations and Networking: Collaborate with other influencers, experts, and bloggers in your niche to expand your reach and enhance your credibility.

Monetization Strategies for Niche Bloggers

Niche bloggers can generate income through various monetization strategies tailored to their audience and niche:

Affiliate Marketing: Promote products or services relevant to your niche and earn a commission for each sale made through your referral links.

Sponsored Content: Partner with brands in your niche for sponsored posts, reviews, or endorsements.

Digital Products: Create and sell e-books, online courses, printables, templates, or other digital resources that cater to your audience's needs.

Membership Sites: Offer premium, exclusive content to subscribers who pay a recurring fee.

Advertising: Monetize through display ads, although this may be more suitable for higher-traffic blogs.

Consulting or Coaching: Leverage your expertise to offer one-on-one consulting or coaching services to your readers.

Event Hosting: Organize webinars, workshops, or live events related to your niche and charge participants a fee.

Building a Strong Brand and Audience Engagement

Niche blogging requires a well-defined brand identity that resonates with your target audience. A cohesive brand encompasses your blog's name, logo, color scheme, and tone of voice. Consistency across all touchpoints helps create a memorable and recognizable brand.

Engagement is essential for building a loyal and active audience. Respond to comments, encourage discussions, and interact with your readers on social media platforms. By fostering a sense of community and making your audience feel valued, you enhance their loyalty and connection to your blog.

Challenges and the Road to Success

Niche blogging comes with its own set of challenges. Niche topics can sometimes have a limited audience, which may impact traffic and income potential. However, a dedicated audience interested in your specific niche tends to be more engaged and likely to convert into customers.

Staying motivated and consistent is vital. Overcoming writer's block, staying updated with industry trends, and managing the demands of content creation can be demanding. The key is to remain passionate about your niche and remember the value you provide to your readers.

Nurturing Expertise and Income in Niche Blogging

Niche blogging is a journey of passion, expertise, and entrepreneurship. By immersing yourself in a specific subject area, you create an opportunity to stand out, connect deeply with your audience, and generate income through various channels. As you navigate this rewarding path, remember that niche blogging is about more than just producing content; it's about nurturing your expertise, fostering a community, and leaving a lasting impact in your chosen niche. With dedication, consistency, and a commitment to delivering value, you can build authority, inspire change, and create a sustainable income stream through the power of niche blogging.

5.   The Power of E-commerce: Launching and Scaling a Successful Online Store

In the digital age, e-commerce has revolutionized the way businesses operate and consumers shop. The ability to establish an online store has democratized entrepreneurship, enabling individuals and businesses of all sizes to reach a global audience and create successful ventures. This exploration delves into the world of e-commerce, uncovering the strategies, challenges, and potential for launching and scaling a thriving online store.

The E-commerce Revolution: Redefining Retail

E-commerce has fundamentally transformed the retail landscape. Traditional brick-and-mortar stores are no longer the sole avenue for purchasing goods. Online stores offer convenience, a vast product selection, and the ability to shop from anywhere, at any time. As a result, consumers have embraced online shopping as a new norm.

The power of e-commerce lies in its accessibility. With platforms and tools readily available, anyone with a product, a passion, or an idea can launch an online store and tap into a global market.

Getting Started: The Foundations of E-commerce

Launching a successful online store requires careful planning, strategic execution, and attention to detail. Here are the essential steps to get started:

Choose Your Niche: Define your target market and choose a niche that aligns with your expertise and passion.

Market Research: Understand your target audience, analyze competitors, and identify trends to inform your product selection and marketing strategy.

Select Your Products: Curate a product catalog that caters to your niche and solves your customers' problems or meets their needs.

Platform Selection: Choose an e-commerce platform (such as Shopify, WooCommerce, or BigCommerce) that suits your business needs and technical comfort level.

Branding and Design: Create a visually appealing and user-friendly website that reflects your brand identity and resonates with your target audience.

Product Listings: Craft compelling product descriptions, showcase high-quality images, and provide all relevant information to enhance the shopping experience.

Payment and Security: Set up secure payment gateways to ensure safe transactions and build customer trust.

Strategies for Success: Building and Scaling

Launching an online store is just the beginning. Scaling your e-commerce business requires a blend of marketing, customer engagement, and strategic decision-making. Here are key strategies for success:

Digital Marketing: Utilize social media, content marketing, email campaigns, and paid advertising to drive traffic to your online store.

Search Engine Optimization (SEO): Optimize your website for search engines to improve visibility and attract organic traffic.

Customer Experience: Provide exceptional customer service, seamless navigation, and a straightforward checkout process.

Data Analysis: Monitor your store's performance using analytics tools to track sales, customer behavior, and identify areas for improvement.

Diversification: Expand your product range, introduce new categories, or offer complementary items to cater to evolving customer needs.

Personalization: Implement strategies like product recommendations and personalized offers to enhance the shopping experience.

Customer Retention: Establish loyalty programs, offer exclusive discounts, and engage with customers through social media and email marketing.

Challenges and Adaptability

E-commerce is not without its challenges. Competition is fierce, consumer expectations are high, and the digital landscape is ever-changing. Staying adaptable and responsive is crucial. You'll need to continuously update your product offerings, refine your marketing strategies, and embrace new technologies to stay ahead.

A New Frontier of Entrepreneurship

E-commerce offers an unparalleled opportunity for entrepreneurs to create, innovate, and scale their businesses. The power to launch a successful online store is within reach, provided you approach it with dedication, strategic planning, and a commitment to delivering value. As you navigate the e-commerce landscape, remember that every challenge is an opportunity for growth, and every customer interaction is a chance to build lasting relationships. With the right mindset and the determination to succeed, you can harness the power of e-commerce to establish a thriving online store and shape the future of your business.

PART III:

INVESTING

OUTSIDE THE BOX

Investing Outside the Box

In the ever-changing landscape of modern finance, where uncertainty and volatility are constants, the traditional adage of "don't put all your eggs in one basket" has never rung truer. As investors strive to achieve a delicate equilibrium between risk and reward, the limitations of relying solely on stocks and bonds as the pillars of their portfolios have become increasingly evident. Enter the realm of alternative investments—a dynamic and diverse universe that extends far beyond the confines of conventional financial instruments. In "Beyond Stocks and Bonds: Alternative Investments for Diversification," we embark on a journey to explore the uncharted territories of investment opportunities, where creativity meets strategy, and where the potential for enhanced returns and risk mitigation is waiting to be unearthed.

This exploration is not merely a departure from the familiar; it is a quest to redefine the very notion of diversification. While traditional assets have proven their worth over time, their interconnectedness and susceptibility to market fluctuations have revealed chinks in the armor of conventional investment wisdom. Our voyage into the world of alternative investments is guided by the belief that true diversification involves embracing a spectrum of choices that extend beyond the surface—choices that have the potential to fortify portfolios against unexpected storms and unlock untapped avenues of growth.

Through these pages, we will unravel the tapestry of alternative investments, shedding light on the various categories that constitute this captivating landscape. From real assets such as real estate and commodities to the intricate dance of private equity and the enigmatic allure of hedge funds, we will delve into the characteristics, risks, and rewards that define each unique corner of this realm. We will confront the challenges head-on, recognizing that every opportunity comes with its own set of considerations, complexities, and potential pitfalls.

In "Beyond Stocks and Bonds," we are not merely spectators observing the evolution of finance; we are active participants in shaping our financial destinies. We'll equip ourselves with the tools to conduct thorough due diligence, make informed decisions, and navigate the uncharted waters of alternative investments with confidence. As the investment landscape continues to evolve, so too does our understanding of risk, return, and resilience. We will explore the symbiotic relationship between traditional and alternative investments, discovering how they can harmonize to create portfolios that not only survive but thrive amidst the tides of change.

As we embark on this intellectual odyssey, keep in mind that the pursuit of knowledge and exploration is a journey, not a destination. Our goal is not to dismiss or replace traditional investments, but to expand our horizons and enrich our investment acumen. "Beyond Stocks and Bonds: Alternative Investments for Diversification" is your passport to a realm where diversification is not just a strategy—it's an art form. So, fasten your seatbelts and open your minds, for the path less traveled promises a wealth of possibilities waiting to be uncovered.

Alternative Investment

In a world where financial markets are evolving at an unprecedented pace and traditional investment options are no longer the sole path to wealth creation, alternative investments have emerged as intriguing avenues for those seeking to diversify their portfolios and explore new horizons. These alternative investments encompass a wide spectrum of options that extend beyond the realm of stocks and bonds, offering unique opportunities for both seasoned investors and those looking to embark on their investment journey.

One such alternative investment that individuals can consider is real estate. Real estate has long been a cornerstone of wealth accumulation, offering the potential for appreciation, rental income, and a hedge against inflation. From residential properties to commercial spaces, real estate investments provide tangible assets that can weather market fluctuations and generate steady returns. Real estate investment trusts (REITs) also offer a way to invest in real estate without the hassle of property management, making it accessible to a broader range of investors.

Private Equity is another avenue that allows individuals to participate in the growth of private companies. This form of investment involves acquiring ownership stakes in non-public companies, often through venture capital, buyouts, or direct investments. While private equity investments typically require a longer holding period and involve higher risks, they can yield substantial returns if successful, as investors benefit from the growth and success of the invested companies.

For those intrigued by financial complexity and skilled risk management, hedge funds present an option. Hedge funds employ a diverse range of investment strategies, from long-short equity trading to macroeconomic speculation, with the aim of generating returns that are uncorrelated with traditional markets. While hedge funds often require higher minimum investments and involve more intricate fee structures, they offer the potential for enhanced diversification and sophisticated risk management techniques.

Commodities and precious metals provide an alternative investment avenue tied to physical assets. These investments can serve as hedges against inflation and currency fluctuations. Commodities like gold, silver, and oil often exhibit low correlation with traditional investments, making them attractive options for diversification.

The world of collectibles and tangible assets also opens up intriguing opportunities. Art, fine wine, rare coins, and other valuable collectibles can appreciate over time and add a touch of passion and personal interest to an investment portfolio. While these investments may require specialized knowledge and due diligence, they can provide a unique blend of financial growth and aesthetic enjoyment.

Moreover, the modern digital age has brought about opportunities in peer-to-peer lending and crowdfunding, where individuals can invest in loans, startups, or real estate projects through online platforms. These avenues offer access to a wide range of investments with potentially attractive returns.

Alternative investments represent a diverse array of options for individuals seeking to expand their investment horizons beyond traditional stocks and bonds. From real estate to private equity, commodities to collectibles, these alternatives offer the potential for enhanced diversification, higher returns, and exposure to unique market dynamics. However, it's important to recognize that alternative investments often come with their own set of risks, complexities, and considerations. Engaging in thorough research, seeking professional guidance, and aligning investments with personal financial goals are critical steps to effectively harness the potential benefits of alternative investments.

The World of Cryptocurrencies: Opportunities and Risks in Digital Assets

Starting with cryptocurrencies can be an exciting and potentially rewarding venture, but it's important to approach it with the right knowledge and mindset. Here's a step-by-step guide on how to get started with cryptocurrencies:

Educate Yourself:

Before diving into the world of cryptocurrencies, take the time to educate yourself. Understand the basic concepts of blockchain technology, how cryptocurrencies work, and the different types of cryptocurrencies available (e.g., Bitcoin, Ethereum, altcoins). There are numerous online resources, articles, forums, and courses that can help you build a solid foundation.

Choose a Cryptocurrency Wallet:

A cryptocurrency wallet is a digital tool used to store, send, and receive cryptocurrencies. There are different types of wallets, including software wallets (desktop, mobile, or online), hardware wallets (physical devices), and paper wallets (physical printouts). Research and choose a wallet that suits your needs and provides a good balance between security and usability.

Select a Cryptocurrency Exchange:

To buy and sell cryptocurrencies, you'll need to sign up for a cryptocurrency exchange. Look for reputable and well-established exchanges that offer a user-friendly interface, a variety of cryptocurrencies, strong security measures, and good customer support. Some popular exchanges include Coinbase, Binance, Kraken, and Gemini.

Complete KYC Verification:

Many exchanges require you to complete a Know Your Customer (KYC) verification process before you can start trading. This involves providing personal information and documentation to verify your identity. KYC helps prevent fraud and ensures compliance with regulations.

Fund Your Account:

Once your exchange account is set up and verified, you can fund it with fiat currency (like USD, EUR, etc.) to buy cryptocurrencies. Exchanges typically offer various payment methods such as bank transfers, credit/debit cards, and even PayPal in some cases.

Start Buying Cryptocurrencies:

With a funded account, you can start buying cryptocurrencies. Choose the cryptocurrency you want to invest in, enter the amount you wish to purchase, review the transaction details, and confirm the purchase. The cryptocurrencies you buy will be stored in your exchange account's wallet.

Practice Security Measures:

Security is paramount in the cryptocurrency world. Use strong and unique passwords, enable two-factor authentication (2FA) for your accounts, and consider using a hardware wallet for added security. Be cautious of phishing scams and only interact with trusted sources.

Explore and Learn:

As you become more comfortable with the basics, explore different aspects of the cryptocurrency space. You can learn about trading strategies, participate in Initial Coin Offerings (ICOs) or token sales (be cautious and do thorough research), experiment with different wallets, and explore decentralized finance (DeFi) platforms.

Stay Updated:

The cryptocurrency space is rapidly evolving, with new developments, technologies, and regulations emerging regularly. Stay updated by following reputable news sources, blogs, social media accounts, and forums related to cryptocurrencies.

Manage Risk and Invest Wisely:

Remember that the cryptocurrency market can be highly volatile. Invest only what you can afford to lose and consider diversifying your investment across different cryptocurrencies. It's a good practice to set clear goals, establish risk management strategies, and avoid making impulsive decisions based on market fluctuations.

Starting with cryptocurrencies requires a combination of knowledge, research, and careful decision-making. By taking the time to educate yourself, practicing good security measures, and approaching your investment journey with a long-term perspective, you can navigate the world of cryptocurrencies with confidence.

OPPORTUNIES IN CRYPTOCURRENCIES

Cryptocurrencies offer a range of opportunities for individuals, investors, and businesses alike. These opportunities stem from the unique characteristics and capabilities of cryptocurrencies and blockchain technology. Here are some of the key opportunities that cryptocurrencies present:

Investment Potential:
Cryptocurrencies have demonstrated the potential for significant price appreciation over time. Early adopters of cryptocurrencies like Bitcoin have seen substantial returns on their investments. Many investors view cryptocurrencies as a way to diversify their investment portfolios and potentially generate higher returns compared to traditional assets.

Portfolio Diversification:

Cryptocurrencies have a low correlation with traditional financial markets, making them an attractive option for diversification. Including cryptocurrencies in a diversified investment portfolio can help reduce overall risk exposure and provide a hedge against market volatility.

Access to New Investment Avenues:

The emergence of Initial Coin Offerings (ICOs) and token sales has opened up opportunities for retail investors to participate in funding early-stage blockchain projects and startups. This democratization of investment access was previously limited to venture capitalists and institutional investors.

Decentralized Finance (DeFi):

DeFi platforms built on blockchain technology offer opportunities for individuals to engage in lending, borrowing, trading, and earning interest on their cryptocurrency holdings without the need for intermediaries. DeFi has the potential to revolutionize traditional financial services by providing greater access, transparency, and control to users.

Global Financial Inclusion:

Cryptocurrencies can provide financial services to unbanked and underbanked populations around the world. People without access to traditional banking systems can use cryptocurrencies to store value, send and receive money, and access financial services via mobile devices.

Innovation and Technological Advancements:

The underlying blockchain technology of cryptocurrencies has applications beyond finance. Blockchain is being explored for supply chain management, identity verification, healthcare, real estate, and more. As these technologies mature, they can drive innovation and efficiency in various industries.

Micropayments and Cross-Border Transactions:
Cryptocurrencies enable fast and low-cost cross-border transactions, especially for micropayments. This is particularly useful for remittances and international commerce, where traditional banking systems can be slow and costly.

Ownership and Digital Assets:
Cryptocurrencies allow for true ownership and transfer of digital assets. This has led to the rise of non-fungible tokens (NFTs), which represent ownership of unique digital items such as art, collectibles, and virtual real estate.

Participation in Blockchain Networks:

Cryptocurrencies often come with governance tokens that allow holders to participate in decision-making processes for blockchain networks. This gives token holders a say in the future development and direction of the platforms they support.

Monetization of Content and Skills:
Cryptocurrencies enable creators and content providers to monetize their work directly from consumers. This can apply to digital art, music, writing, and other creative endeavors without relying on traditional intermediaries.

While cryptocurrencies offer exciting opportunities, it's important to note that they also come with risks, including price volatility, regulatory uncertainties, and security concerns. As with any investment, careful research, risk management, and a long-term perspective are crucial when exploring opportunities in the world of cryptocurrencies.

Impact Investing: Making Money with a Social and Environmental Conscience

Making money with a social and environmental conscience, often referred to as impact investing or socially responsible investing, involves aligning your financial goals with ethical considerations and positive societal impact. This approach allows you to generate returns while contributing to causes you believe in. Here's a guide on how to make money with a social and environmental conscience:

1. Define Your Values and Goals:

Start by identifying the social and environmental issues that matter most to you. Consider whether you want to focus on clean energy, sustainable agriculture, gender equality, poverty alleviation, or other specific causes. Clarify your long-term goals, whether they involve maximizing financial returns, creating positive impact, or finding a balance between the two.

2. Research and Educate Yourself:

Gain a deep understanding of the issues you're passionate about and how they intersect with financial markets. Learn about different investment options, strategies, and financial instruments that align with your values. Read books, attend workshops, and follow reputable sources to stay informed.

3. Explore Impact Investments:

Impact investments are designed to generate positive social or environmental outcomes alongside financial returns. Look for companies, funds, or projects that prioritize sustainability, social responsibility, and ethical practices. These could include renewable energy projects, sustainable agriculture initiatives, affordable housing developments, and more.

4. Consider Socially Responsible Funds:

Many investment firms offer socially responsible funds that pool money from multiple investors to invest in companies with positive social and environmental practices. Research different funds, evaluate their track records, and understand their investment strategies before making a decision.

5. Evaluate Companies and Investments:

Conduct thorough due diligence on potential investments. Examine a company's environmental, social, and governance (ESG) performance to assess its commitment to sustainability and responsible business practices. Look for transparent reporting and clear alignment with your values.

6. Engage in Shareholder Activism:

If you invest in publicly traded companies, consider engaging in shareholder activism by voting on key issues, attending shareholder meetings, and collaborating with other socially conscious investors to influence positive change within companies.

7. Explore Community Investments:

Community investments support local businesses and projects that have a positive impact on the surrounding community. These could include affordable housing developments, community gardens, microfinance initiatives, and more.

8. Diversify Your Portfolio:

Just like traditional investing, diversification is important. Spread your investments across different sectors, asset classes, and regions to manage risk and enhance the potential for stable returns.

9. Monitor and Measure Impact:

Regularly assess the impact of your investments by tracking key metrics and outcomes related to your chosen causes. Many impact investments provide metrics that measure their social and environmental performance.

10. Stay Informed and Evolve:

The landscape of impact investing is constantly evolving. Stay up to date with emerging trends, regulations, and innovations in the field. Adapt your investment strategy as needed to continue aligning with your values and maximizing impact.

Remember that making money with a social and environmental conscience requires a long-term perspective and a commitment to both financial returns and positive change. By carefully selecting investments that align with your values and actively engaging with your investment choices, you can create a meaningful and impactful financial portfolio.

Real Estate Ventures: Exploring Creative Ways to Invest in Property

The following is a suitable real estate definition: a real estate category with physical assets. This includes any land, structures built thereon, and land enhancements like a road or personal well.

Real estate also includes the owner's right to use the land and its improvements as they like. Real estate includes land features including waterways, forests, and mineral resources. Even if the land is sold to someone else, the original landowner may occasionally decide to keep the rights to certain features.

Why real estate then?

Real estate has the potential to provide a great return on investment, therefore you might want to consider doing so. The investment is far less volatile than the stock market. It also has true worth. In contrast to equities, which can fall to pennies on the dollar, real estate always has value.

As an alternative, you might prefer to work as a real estate agent due of its advantages. Real estate agents claim to appreciate their work and love being able to assist others. Agents in the real estate industry have a lot of opportunity for revenue.

Of course, many people also dream of owning their own piece of property. The American dream and the dream of people in other countries throughout the world both include owning your own home. Real estate has one of the highest rates of value growth of any investments. Owning a business is a good option if you want to use the economy to increase your wealth.

Five Ways to Start Investing in Real Estate

1.   Purchase real estate investment trusts (REITs)

You can invest in real estate through REITs even if you don't own any actual property. They are businesses that own commercial real estate, such as office buildings, retail spaces, apartments, and hotels. They are frequently compared to mutual funds. Due to their propensity for paying substantial dividends, REITs are a popular choice for retirement investments. Investors can automatically reinvest those dividends to increase the value of their investment if they do not want or desire the regular income.

Arc REITs a wise financial choice? While they might be, they might also be varied and complex. Some are not publicly traded, while others are exchanged on an exchange like stocks. Given that non-traded REITs are difficult to sell and may be difficult to evaluate, the type of REIT you choose to invest in can have a significant impact on the level of risk you assume. In general, novice investors should stick to publicly traded REITs, which you may buy through brokerage companies.

You will require a brokerage account for that. Opening one, if you don't already have one, takes less than 15 minutes, and many companies don't demand an initial investment (though the REIT itself probably will).

By investing in a fund that holds holdings in numerous REITs, you can also expose yourself to a more diverse variety of real estate investments. This could be accomplished by purchasing shares of a mutual fund that contains REITs or by investing in a real estate exchange-traded fund (ETF).

2. Make use of an internet real estate investing tool

Developers of real estate can connect with investors who are looking to fund projects with debt or equity through real estate investment platforms. In return for assuming a sizable level of risk and paying a fee to the platform, investors anticipate receiving monthly or quarterly payments. These are speculative and illiquid investments, similar to many real estate ones, and are difficult to sell the way stocks are.

The catch is that you could require money in order to make money. Many of these platforms are only accessible to accredited investors, which are those who have earned more than $200,000 ($300,000 with a spouse) per year in income or have a net worth of at least $1 million, excluding their primary residence, according to the Securities and Exchange Commission. Fundrise and RealtyMogul are options for people who are unable to achieve that stipulation.

3. Consider purchasing real estate to rent out.

When she made the decision to purchase her first rental property at the age of 21, Tiffany Alexy had no intention of becoming a real estate investor. She thought purchasing would be preferable to renting while she was a senior in college in Raleigh, North Carolina. She intended to attend graduate school nearby.

"I looked on Craigslist and discovered a four-bedroom, four-bath condo that was furnished in a manner reminiscent of student accommodation. I purchased it, lived in one bedroom, and rented the other three out, recalls Alexy.

The arrangement paid for all of her costs and provided an additional $100 in cash each month; for a graduate student, this was far from pocket change and was sufficient for Alexy to become fixated on real estate.

The term "house hacking," which was coined by BiggerPockets, an online resource for real estate speculators, was used by Alexy to enter the market. It simply means that you are inhabiting your investment property, either by renting out individual units in a multi-unit complex, as Alexy did, or by renting out rooms, as Alexy did. House hacking allows investors to purchase a property with up to four units and still be eligible for a residential loan, according to David Meyer, vice president of data and analytics at the website.

Of course, it's also possible to purchase an entire investment property and rent it out. Find one whose combined costs are less than the most you can charge for rent. Additionally, if you don't want to be the one to arrive at the scene of a leak with a toolbelt - You will also have to pay a property manager, or even the person who makes the call.

4.   Think   about   renovating   investment properties

This is HGTV in real life: You invest in a home that is underpriced and in need of some TLC, restore it on a budget, and then flip it for a profit. The tactic, known as house flipping, is slightly more difficult than it appears on television. Given the current greater cost of building materials and mortgage interest rates, it is also more expensive than it was in the past. Many people who flip houses want to pay cash for them.

"There is a bigger element of risk," says Meyer, "because so much of the math behind flipping requires a very accurate estimate of how much repairs are going to cost, which is not an easy thing to do."

Find a partner with experience, he advised. "Perhaps you have resources to contribute, like money or time, but you find a contractor who is good at budgeting or project management," he says.

The other risk of flipping is that you could lose money if you hold the home for an extended period of time since you would have to pay the mortgage without receiving any revenue. By residing in the house while it is being renovated, you can reduce that risk. As long as the most of the upgrades are cosmetic and you don't mind a little dust, this works.

5. Hire a space

You might also consider renting out a portion of your house to dip a toe in the real estate waters. It may be possible for people to continue living in their homes while still enjoying the price gain on their property thanks to an arrangement like this that significantly lowers housing costs.

For younger folks, getting a roommate can help lower their monthly mortgage cost. Try a website like Airbnb instead if you're unsure of your readiness. It's house hacking for people who don't like commitments because you don't have to take on a long-term tenant, Airbnb at least partially screens possible tenants, and the host guarantee offered by the firm covers any damages.

Comparing renting a room to the sophisticated idea of real estate investing, renting a room feels much more approachable. You can rent a room if you have one.

The finest real estate investments, like all other investment choices, are those that best benefit you, the investor. Consider how much time you have, how much money you're prepared to spend, and whether you want to be the one who handles domestic issues when they inevitably arise. Instead of investing directly in a property if you lack DIY abilities, think about using a REIT or a crowdfunding platform to invest in real estate.

PART IV:
EMBRACING THE
REMOTE WORK
LIFESTYLE

Remote Work Revolution: Unlocking the Benefits of Location Independence

The privilege of working remotely, which was formerly reserved for millennial bloggers and vloggers, is now firmly expanding to a larger range of businesses and sorts of labor. More and more people are choosing to work remotely because it gives them the freedom to live more flexible lifestyles, be more productive at work, and pick up new skills in the process.

But things are not always easy. And it's definitely not as straightforward as simply bringing everything off your office desk. The obstacles of remote work, which have an influence on our mental, physical, and emotional wellbeing, come along with the 56% of organizations that are now receptive to the idea.

Fortunately, if you decide to start working remotely, there are many ways to get over each of these difficulties.

A few of the most well-known companies, including Twitter, Facebook, and Coinbase, have declared that all of their staff members are now able to work from home on a regular basis. However, simply choosing to switch is not enough. One of the frequent difficulties of working remotely is the tendency to believe that everything can or ought to remain the same. The exact opposite is true, in fact.

Currently, you might use the office walls for group brainstorming or hold a monthly show-and-tell demo in a single room with the entire department. You might be the type of person who prefers to get up and speak to your coworkers face-to-face rather than using instant messaging services like Slack or Skype.

These are only a few of the (more) visible modes of working that are obviously unsustainable when remote workers do their business from home. The greatest advice for overcoming the obstacles of remote work is to effectively start over: Treat it as if you have a new team or are beginning a new position at a different organization.

If you are the team's manager or team leader, it may be your responsibility to establish new working procedures that will be more convenient for everyone and to provide your response to issues from remote workers some structure.

Have essential talks about your future working agreements, the meetings you must hold and when, the methods you will use to document, exchange, and communicate, and the things that will be important to consider.

Before making the change, it's crucial to resolve these issues. Nevertheless, the guiding principle in this situation is to not assume that working life would remain the same.

CHALLENGES OF REMOTE WORK

The drawbacks of working remotely outweigh all the benefits, and there are a variety of issues that come up. Unplugging after work, which 22% of respondents indicated they encounter, is the most typical challenge faced by remote employees, according to Buffer's State of Remote Work survey.

1. The Isolation Quandary:

One of the most significant challenges of working remotely is the sense of isolation that can creep in. Gone are the days of spontaneous office interactions, coffee breaks, and face-to-face meetings. This isolation can lead to feelings of loneliness, reduced social interactions, and even potential impacts on mental health. To counter this challenge, individuals and organizations must prioritize building and maintaining strong virtual connections through regular video calls, virtual team-building activities, and open communication channels.

2. Balancing Work and Life:

While remote work offers flexibility, it can also blur the lines between professional and personal life. Without a clear separation between workspace and living space, individuals may find it challenging to switch off from work, leading to burnout and decreased well-being. Creating a dedicated workspace and establishing clear boundaries for work hours can help maintain a healthy work-life balance.

3. Communication Complexities:

Effective communication is the backbone of any successful endeavor, and remote work introduces new challenges in this arena. Digital communication lacks the nuance of in-person interactions, leading to potential misinterpretations and misunderstandings. To address this, organizations should encourage transparent and frequent communication, promote the use of video calls whenever possible, and provide training on virtual communication etiquette.

4. Distractions and Productivity:

The home environment, while comfortable, can also be rife with distractions that impede productivity. Household chores, family members, and personal devices can all divert attention from work tasks. Developing strong time management skills, setting clear priorities, and creating a dedicated and organized workspace can help mitigate distractions and enhance overall productivity.

5. Technology Trials and Tribulations:

Reliant on digital tools and technology, remote work is susceptible to technical glitches, internet connectivity issues, and software malfunctions. These disruptions can lead to delays, frustration, and hampered collaboration. To overcome this challenge, individuals should familiarize themselves with the tools they use, maintain regular updates, and have contingency plans in place to address technical challenges swiftly.

6. Loss of Company Culture:

Company culture often thrives on in-person interactions and shared experiences. In a remote work setup, maintaining and fostering a strong company culture can be a challenge. Organizations should invest in virtual team-building activities, create opportunities for social interactions, and ensure that core values and goals are communicated effectively across remote teams.

7. Career Advancement and Visibility:

Remote work may impact an individual's visibility within the organization, potentially affecting opportunities for career advancement and recognition. To address this challenge, remote workers should actively seek opportunities to showcase their skills, contribute to projects, and engage with colleagues and supervisors to ensure that their contributions are acknowledged and valued.

While remote work offers unparalleled freedom and flexibility, it also presents a unique set of challenges that demand proactive solutions. By acknowledging these challenges and implementing strategies to address them, individuals and organizations can navigate the remote work landscape successfully. With effective communication, a focus on well-being, and a commitment to maintaining strong connections, remote work can indeed be a transformative and rewarding experience for all involved.

Digital Nomadism: Traveling and Making Money Simultaneously

Digital Nomadism: Embracing a Life of Adventure and Earning While You Roam

Imagine waking up to the sound of waves crashing on a tropical beach, sipping your morning coffee as you watch the sunrise over a bustling city skyline, or exploring ancient ruins in a far-off land. Now, picture doing all of this while simultaneously earning a living. This is the essence of digital nomadism – a lifestyle that merges work and travel, allowing individuals to explore the world while pursuing their professional ambitions. In this article, we dive into the concept of digital nomadism, its allure, challenges, and how to embark on this exciting journey.

1. The Rise of Digital Nomadism:

Digital nomadism has emerged as a paradigm shift in the traditional work landscape. Enabled by the advent of technology, remote work, and an increasingly interconnected world, individuals are no longer confined to a specific location to earn a living. Instead, they leverage digital tools, the internet, and their skills to work from anywhere they choose.

2. The Allure of the Digital Nomad Lifestyle:

The appeal of digital nomadism is undeniable. It offers the freedom to explore diverse cultures, experience new landscapes, and create a life rich in experiences. Whether it's immersing oneself in a bustling metropolis, retreating to tranquil nature, or navigating the winding alleys of a historic village, digital nomads can tailor their surroundings to suit their preferences.

3. Challenges and Realities:

While the digital nomad lifestyle paints a captivating picture, it's essential to recognize that it comes with its own set of challenges. Fluctuating time zones, potential feelings of isolation, and the need for self-discipline are just a few aspects that require careful consideration. The quest for reliable internet connections and managing work-life balance in the midst of exploration can also present hurdles.

4. Making Money on the Move:

Digital nomads sustain their lifestyle by utilizing their skills and expertise to earn an income online. Freelancing, remote work arrangements, entrepreneurship, and digital marketing are popular avenues. Thanks to the internet, a diverse range of professions – from writing, design, and coding to online teaching and consulting – can be seamlessly carried out from anywhere with a reliable internet connection.

5. Embracing the Digital Nomad Lifestyle:

For those eager to embark on a journey of digital nomadism, a few key steps can set them on the right path:

6. **Skill Development:** Hone skills that are conducive to remote work, such as coding, graphic design, writing, or digital marketing.

7. **Build an Online Presence:** Establish a strong online presence through a professional website,

social media platforms, and an engaging portfolio to attract clients and opportunities.

8. **Remote Work Opportunities:** Explore remote job listings on platforms tailored for digital nomads, or propose remote work arrangements with current employers.

9. **Freelancing and Entrepreneurship**: Venture into freelancing platforms or launch a digital business that aligns with your expertise and passions.

10. **Plan and Budget:** Carefully plan your travel destinations, accommodation, and expenses to ensure a sustainable lifestyle.

11. **Stay Connected:** Prioritize staying connected with fellow digital nomads and building a supportive network to share experiences, tips, and insights.

Digital nomadism is not just a lifestyle; it's a mindset that embraces adventure, flexibility, and the limitless possibilities of the digital age. By combining work and travel, individuals can unlock a world of enriching experiences, broaden their horizons, and create a life that harmonizes professional success with personal fulfillment. As technology continues to evolve and the remote work landscape expands, the allure of the digital nomad lifestyle is likely to grow, offering a transformative way to live, work, and explore the global tapestry of cultures and landscapes.

Working in the Cloud: Thriving in the Virtual Workspace

In the ever-evolving landscape of modern work, a transformative phenomenon has taken center stage – working in the cloud. The convergence of advanced technology, remote collaboration tools, and the shift toward remote work has given rise to a virtual workspace that transcends traditional office boundaries. This article delves into the concept of working in the cloud, exploring its benefits, challenges, and strategies for thriving in this dynamic and interconnected environment.

The Essence of Working in the Cloud:

Working in the cloud, often referred to as cloud-based work or remote work, involves utilizing digital platforms, applications, and online tools to perform tasks, collaborate with colleagues, and conduct business operations. Instead of being tethered to a physical office, individuals leverage the power of the cloud to access their work from anywhere with an internet connection.

Benefits of Embracing the Virtual Workspace:

The virtual workspace offers a myriad of advantages that redefine the way we approach work:

1. Flexibility: Working in the cloud allows for flexibility in terms of location and work hours. Individuals can choose when and where they work, fostering a healthier work-life balance.

2. Global Collaboration: Geographical barriers dissolve as teams collaborate seamlessly across time zones and borders, leveraging cloud-based tools for communication and project management.

3. Cost Efficiency: Organizations can save on overhead costs associated with maintaining physical office spaces, while individuals can reduce commuting expenses.

4. Increased Productivity: Cloud-based tools offer real-time collaboration and accessibility to documents, enhancing productivity and reducing delays.

5.   Access to Talent: Businesses can tap into a global talent pool, sourcing specialized skills regardless of their physical location.

6.   Navigating Challenges in the Virtual Workspace:
While the cloud-based work environment offers remarkable benefits, it also presents unique challenges that require adaptability and strategic solutions:

1. Communication and Collaboration: Ensuring effective communication can be challenging, as digital interactions lack the nuances of face-to-face conversations. Utilizing video conferencing, instant messaging, and project management tools is essential.

2. Data Security and Privacy: Protecting sensitive information is a concern in the digital realm. Employing robust cybersecurity measures and

encryption protocols is crucial to safeguarding data.

3. Isolation and Engagement: Working remotely can lead to feelings of isolation and disconnection. Employers must actively foster a sense of belonging through virtual team-building activities and regular check-ins.

4. Maintaining Work-Life Boundaries: The lines between work and personal life can blur in the virtual workspace. Establishing clear boundaries and routines helps prevent burnout.

Strategies for Thriving in the Cloud:

To thrive in the virtual workspace, individuals and organizations can consider the following strategies:

1. Embrace Technology: Familiarize yourself with cloud-based tools for communication,

collaboration, and project management to optimize workflow.

2. Establish a Routine: Create a structured routine that includes designated work hours, breaks, and leisure time to maintain a healthy work-life balance.

3. Communication Protocols: Set clear communication expectations and protocols to ensure everyone is on the same page and reduce misunderstandings.

4. Virtual Team Building: Organize virtual team-building activities and social interactions to foster a sense of community and camaraderie.

5. Continuous Learning: Stay updated on the latest technological advancements and best practices to maximize productivity and efficiency.

Working in the cloud represents a paradigm shift that empowers individuals and organizations to transcend the limitations of physical space and embrace a new era of work. By leveraging the benefits of cloud-based tools, addressing challenges proactively, and adopting strategies for success, individuals and teams can not only navigate the virtual workspace but thrive in an interconnected and dynamic work environment. The cloud is not just a platform; it's a gateway to innovation, collaboration, and a future where work knows no geographical bounds.

Freelancing Platforms and Remote Job Opportunities: Navigating the Path to Your Niche

In the rapidly evolving landscape of work, traditional career paths are making way for a world of freelancing and remote job opportunities. The rise of digital platforms has empowered individuals to showcase their skills and expertise to a global audience, while organizations are tapping into a vast talent pool regardless of geographical boundaries. This article delves into the realm of freelancing platforms and remote job opportunities, guiding you through the process of finding your niche in this dynamic and interconnected landscape.

The Freelancing Revolution:

Freelancing has emerged as a transformative force, offering professionals the freedom to work on projects of their choosing, set their own schedules, and collaborate with clients and companies from around the world. As traditional employment models shift, freelancing platforms have become the virtual marketplace connecting talent with opportunities.

Exploring Freelancing Platforms:

Freelancing platforms act as digital marketplaces where individuals can offer their skills and services to a diverse range of clients. These platforms provide an array of job categories, enabling freelancers to discover their niche and showcase their expertise. Whether you're a writer, designer, developer, marketer, or consultant, there's a platform suited to your skills.

Benefits of Freelancing Platforms:

Global Reach: Freelancing platforms offer access to a global clientele, allowing you to work with clients from different industries, cultures, and time zones.

Portfolio Building: Establish a compelling online portfolio showcasing your work, testimonials, and accomplishments to attract potential clients.

Flexible Work Arrangements: Choose projects that align with your skills, interests, and availability, granting you the flexibility to create your own work-life balance.

Income Diversification: Freelancing allows you to diversify your income streams by taking on multiple projects from different clients.

Navigating the Remote Job Landscape:
Remote job opportunities have gained traction as organizations embrace the benefits of a distributed workforce. Whether you're seeking a full-time remote position or part-time freelancing gigs, the remote job landscape offers a wealth of possibilities.

Identifying Your Niche:
Discovering your niche is a pivotal step in the freelancing and remote job journey. Here's how to pinpoint your area of expertise:

Self-Assessment: Reflect on your skills, interests, and passions. Identify the areas where you excel and the tasks you genuinely enjoy.

Market Research: Investigate the demand for your skills within the freelancing platforms or remote job market. Analyze which niches are thriving and align with your strengths.

Skill Enhancement: Invest in continuous learning to hone your skills and stay current in your chosen niche.

Crafting Your Profile:
Your online profile on freelancing platforms is your digital storefront. Optimize it to stand out:

Create a Compelling Bio: Craft a succinct yet engaging bio that highlights your skills, experience, and what sets you apart.

Showcase Your Portfolio: Display samples of your best work to demonstrate your capabilities to potential clients.

Leverage Keywords: Use relevant keywords in your profile to improve visibility and attract relevant job offers.

Building Your Reputation:
Reputation is paramount in the freelancing world. Deliver exceptional work, communicate effectively, and cultivate positive relationships with clients to earn positive reviews and repeat business.

Networking and Growth:
Participate in freelancing communities, forums, and social media groups related to your niche. Networking not only expands your professional circle but also opens doors to new opportunities and collaborations.

Freelancing platforms and remote job opportunities offer a gateway to a flexible and rewarding career path. By identifying your niche, crafting a standout profile, and delivering top-notch work, you can navigate the virtual landscape with confidence.

Whether you're a writer, designer, programmer, or consultant, the digital realm is brimming with potential for you to showcase your skills, connect with clients, and create a thriving career on your terms.

PART V: PURSUING PASSION PROJECTS

Passion as a Currency: Transforming Your Unique Interests and Talents into Income

In a world brimming with opportunities and fueled by innovation, the concept of currency has expanded beyond traditional forms of money. Today, passion has emerged as a valuable currency, offering individuals the ability to monetize their unique interests and talents in ways that were once unthinkable. This article explores the profound idea of passion as a currency, guiding you on a journey to transform your passions into a source of income and fulfillment.

Unveiling the Power of Passion:

Passion is the driving force behind human creativity, innovation, and personal fulfillment. It's that spark that ignites your soul and fuels your pursuits, whether it's painting, writing, cooking, or crafting. In a digital age that thrives on authenticity and individuality, your passions are a unique asset that can be leveraged to create meaningful and profitable endeavors.

The Path to Monetization:

1. Discover Your Passion: Start by identifying your genuine interests and talents. Reflect on activities that bring you joy, energize you, and make you lose track of time.

2. Unearth Opportunities: Explore how your passion can be transformed into a viable

income stream. Research market trends, demand, and potential avenues for monetization.

3. Craft Your Niche: Define your niche within your chosen passion. This could involve specializing in a specific style of art, a unique cooking technique, or a distinct writing voice.

4. Develop Your Skills: Dedicate time to honing your skills and continuously improving. Seek out training, courses, and mentorship to enhance your expertise.

Monetization Strategies:

1. Freelancing and Consulting: Offer your services as a freelancer or consultant in your chosen niche. Whether it's designing logos, providing financial advice, or offering fitness coaching, your

expertise can be monetized through individual clients or businesses.

2.   Content Creation: Create valuable content in the form of blog posts, videos, podcasts, or social media posts. Build an audience and monetize your content through advertising, sponsorships, or crowdfunding.

3.   E-commerce and Artisan Crafts: Turn your creative passions into tangible products. Whether it's handmade jewelry, custom artwork, or personalized crafts, e-commerce platforms provide a global marketplace to sell your creations.

4.   Courses and Workshops: Share your knowledge and skills through online courses, workshops, or webinars. Platforms like Udemy, Teachable, or Skillshare offer opportunities to monetize your expertise.

5.   Affiliate Marketing: Partner with brands and promote products or services related to your passion. Earn commissions for each sale or referral generated through your promotional efforts.

Cultivating a Passion-Driven Mindset:

1.   Believe in Your Worth: Recognize the value of your passion and expertise. Price your products or services accordingly, reflecting the unique value you bring.

2.   Embrace Continuous Learning: Stay curious and committed to growth. Invest in learning experiences that expand your knowledge and enhance your offerings.

3.   Network and Collaborate: Connect with like-minded individuals, potential clients, and fellow passion-preneurs. Collaboration can open doors to new opportunities and widen your reach.

4.   Stay Resilient: Building a passion-based business requires dedication and perseverance. Embrace challenges as learning experiences and use setbacks as stepping stones toward success.

5.   Passion is a currency that transcends monetary value, enriching both your life and the lives of those you touch. By embracing your unique interests and talents, you have the power to transform your passion into a meaningful and sustainable source of income. Whether you're an artist, a chef, a writer, or an adventurer, the journey of monetizing your passion is a testament to the boundless potential of human creativity and the remarkable possibilities that arise when passion becomes the driving force behind your endeavors.

In a world where innovation and imagination intersect, the realm of arts and culture has become a dynamic playground for entrepreneurs. Arts and culture entrepreneurship involves harnessing creativity to not only create meaningful and impactful works but also to build thriving businesses. This article delves into the captivating world of arts and culture entrepreneurship, exploring how individuals can navigate the fusion of artistic passion and entrepreneurial acumen to carve out successful paths in this diverse landscape.

The Intersection of Art and Entrepreneurship:

Arts and culture entrepreneurship is a convergence of artistic expression and business savvy. It's the art of transforming ideas, talents, and creativity into sustainable ventures that resonate with audiences, while also generating revenue and fostering innovation.

Key Pillars of Arts and Culture Entrepreneurship:

1.   Creative Vision: Entrepreneurs in the arts and culture sector begin with a clear creative vision. This

vision serves as the foundation upon which their business is built, guiding their artistic direction and strategic decisions.

2. Business Acumen: Creativity alone isn't enough; entrepreneurs need business skills to navigate the challenges of marketing, financing, operations, and scaling their ventures.

3. Audience Engagement: Successful arts and culture entrepreneurs understand their target audience and tailor their offerings to captivate and engage their viewers, readers, listeners, or patrons.

4. Innovation: Innovation is a hallmark of arts and culture entrepreneurship. Entrepreneurs must continually evolve and adapt their creative offerings to remain relevant in a rapidly changing landscape.

Navigating the Arts and Culture Entrepreneurial Landscape:

1.   Identify Your Niche: Discover your unique artistic style or form of expression that sets you apart. This could be anything from visual arts, performing arts, literature, design, fashion, or any other creative pursuit.

2.   Market Research: Understand your target audience, their preferences, and their needs. Conduct market research to identify gaps and opportunities in the arts and culture sector.

3.   Business Plan: Craft a comprehensive business plan that outlines your creative goals, target audience, revenue streams, marketing strategies, and operational plans.

4.   Branding and Promotion: Develop a strong brand identity that reflects your artistic vision. Utilize social media, online platforms, and networking to promote your work and connect with your audience.

5.   Collaboration: Collaborate with other artists, cultural organizations, and creative professionals. Collaborations can amplify your reach and bring fresh perspectives to your projects.

Monetization Strategies for Artists and Creatives:

1.   Sell Artwork: Offer your art pieces for sale through galleries, online marketplaces, and exhibitions.

2.   Commissions: Accept commissions for custom artworks, designs, or creative projects tailored to clients' preferences.

3.   Workshops and Classes: Share your expertise by offering workshops, classes, or online courses that teach others your artistic techniques.

4.	Licensing and Merchandising: License your artwork for use on products such as clothing, accessories, and home decor.

5.	Public Speaking and Consulting: Leverage your creative expertise to provide insights, advice, or presentations at events, conferences, and organizations.

Cultivating Success in Arts and Culture Entrepreneurship:

1.	Passion and Persistence: A strong passion for your craft and an unwavering commitment to your artistic vision are vital for overcoming challenges.

2.	Continuous Learning: Stay updated on industry trends, artistic techniques, and business strategies to remain innovative and relevant.

3.   Adaptability: Be open to adapting your creative approach and business strategies based on feedback and changing market demands.

4.   Building Networks: Forge connections within the arts and culture community, collaborate with peers, and build relationships with potential clients and partners.

Arts and culture entrepreneurship represents the fusion of artistry and business prowess, a realm where creativity and innovation intertwine with entrepreneurial spirit. By embracing your artistic passion, honing your business skills, and connecting with your audience, you can navigate this captivating landscape and build a successful venture that not only reflects your unique creative expression but also resonates with the hearts and minds of those who engage with your work. Whether you're a visual artist, a performer, a writer, or a designer, the journey of arts and culture entrepreneurship is a testament to the boundless potential of combining artistry and enterprise.

Non-Profit and Social Entrepreneurship: Merging Impact and Income for Positive Change

In a world where social responsibility and entrepreneurship converge, the realms of non-profit and social entrepreneurship have emerged as powerful catalysts for creating positive impact while generating sustainable income. This article delves into the inspiring landscape of non-profit and social entrepreneurship, exploring how these ventures combine purpose-driven missions with innovative business strategies to address societal challenges and drive meaningful change.

Defining Non-Profit and Social Entrepreneurship:

Non-profit organizations and social entrepreneurs share a common goal: to make a difference in the world. However, they do so through distinct approaches:

- Non-Profit Organizations: These entities are driven by a mission to address social, environmental, or community needs. They reinvest their resources into their cause rather than distributing profits to stakeholders.

- Social Entrepreneurship: Social entrepreneurs leverage business principles to create sustainable solutions for social problems. They focus on generating both social impact and financial returns.

Key Pillars of Non-Profit and Social Entrepreneurship:

- Purpose-Driven Mission: Both non-profits and social entrepreneurs are fueled by a clear and compelling mission aimed at creating positive change and addressing a specific societal challenge.

- Innovation: Social entrepreneurship emphasizes innovative approaches and business models to achieve social impact while ensuring financial viability.

- Sustainability: While non-profits rely on donations and grants, social entrepreneurs strive for financial sustainability by creating revenue-generating streams that support their social goals.

- Collaboration: Non-profits and social entrepreneurs often collaborate with diverse stakeholders, including government agencies, businesses, and communities, to amplify their impact.

Navigating the Landscape of Non-Profit and Social Entrepreneurship:

- Identify a Social Issue: Begin by identifying a pressing social issue that aligns with your passion and expertise. Conduct thorough research to understand its root causes and potential solutions.

- Craft a Vision: Develop a clear and inspiring vision for your non-profit organization or social enterprise, outlining your objectives, strategies, and anticipated impact.

- Business Model Innovation: Social entrepreneurs need to design innovative business models that generate revenue while furthering their social mission. This could involve product sales, services, partnerships, or a combination of revenue streams.

- Strategic Partnerships: Collaborate with like-minded organizations, businesses, and individuals to leverage resources, expand your reach, and enhance your impact.

Monetization Strategies for Non-Profits and Social Entrepreneurs:

- Donations and Grants: Non-profit organizations rely on charitable donations and grants from individuals, corporations, and foundations.

- Social Enterprises: Social entrepreneurs generate income through product sales, service offerings, or unique business models that align with their mission.

- Crowdfunding: Utilize online crowdfunding platforms to raise funds from a diverse community of supporters who believe in your cause.

- Impact Investment: Attract investors who are committed to both financial returns and social impact by offering opportunities to invest in your mission.

Cultivating Success in Non-Profit and Social Entrepreneurship:

- Authenticity and Transparency: Maintain unwavering authenticity and transparency in all your endeavors, earning the trust and support of your stakeholders.

- Measurable Impact: Establish clear metrics to measure and communicate the tangible impact of your initiatives, demonstrating accountability to your supporters.

- Continuous Learning: Stay informed about the latest developments in your field, continuously learning and adapting your strategies to remain effective.

- Resilience and Adaptability: Address challenges with resilience and adaptability, pivoting your approach when necessary to overcome obstacles.

Non-profit and social entrepreneurship exemplify the harmonious fusion of purpose and profit, where societal challenges are met with innovative solutions that create positive change while ensuring financial sustainability. By embracing a mission-driven mindset, designing innovative business models, and collaborating with diverse stakeholders, non-profit organizations and social entrepreneurs can amplify their impact and create a brighter future for communities and causes around the world. Whether you're driven by social justice, environmental conservation, or community empowerment, the journey of non-profit and social entrepreneurship is a testament to the boundless potential of combining compassion and business acumen to shape a better world.

Innovative Funding Models: Exploring Crowdfunding and Beyond for Your Ventures

In a rapidly evolving financial landscape, traditional funding models are being complemented and, in some cases, even replaced by innovative approaches that harness the power of technology, community, and creativity. Crowdfunding is at the forefront of this revolution, but it's just one facet of a broader spectrum of funding options available to entrepreneurs and visionaries. This article delves into the world of innovative funding models, spotlighting crowdfunding and exploring other creative avenues to finance your ventures.

The Rise of Crowdfunding:

Crowdfunding has democratized the process of raising funds for projects, products, and initiatives. It empowers individuals, startups, and organizations to source contributions from a large number of people, often in exchange for rewards, equity, or simply the satisfaction of supporting a cause.

Key Types of Crowdfunding:

- Reward-Based Crowdfunding: Backers contribute funds in exchange for non-monetary rewards such as products, experiences, or early access.

- Equity Crowdfunding: Investors receive ownership shares in the venture in exchange for their financial support.

- Donation-Based Crowdfunding: Supporters make contributions without expecting any financial return, typically to support charitable, artistic, or social projects.

- Debt Crowdfunding (Peer-to-Peer Lending): Entrepreneurs borrow money from a crowd of lenders and repay it with interest over time.

Beyond Crowdfunding:

- While crowdfunding is a powerful tool, it's important to explore other innovative funding models that can complement or extend your fundraising efforts.

- Venture Capital and Angel Investors: For startups with high growth potential, seeking venture capital or angel investment offers access to expertise, mentorship, and substantial financial support.

- Accelerators and Incubators: These programs provide startups with funding, resources, and guidance in exchange for equity. They often come with mentorship and networking opportunities.

- Revenue-Based Financing: This model involves investors providing capital in exchange for a share of future revenues. It offers flexible repayment based on business performance.

- Cryptocurrency and Blockchain Funding: Initial Coin Offerings (ICOs) and Security Token Offerings (STOs) leverage blockchain technology to raise funds by issuing digital tokens.

- Impact Investment: Impact investors fund ventures that generate positive social or environmental impact alongside financial returns.

- Bootstrapping: Entrepreneurs fund their ventures using personal savings, revenue from sales, or minimal external financing.

- Government Grants and Subsidies: Many governments offer grants, subsidies, or tax incentives to support startups and initiatives in specific industries.

Choosing the Right Funding Model:

- Alignment with Mission: Select a funding model that aligns with your venture's goals, values, and vision.

- Stage of Development: Different funding models are suitable for various stages of development, from seed funding to growth and expansion.

- Risk Tolerance: Consider your risk tolerance and willingness to give up ownership or repay funds under different funding structures.

- Investor Compatibility: Build relationships with investors who share your vision and can offer strategic guidance.

Crafting a Successful Fundraising Strategy:

- Clear Value Proposition: Clearly articulate the value and potential impact of your venture to attract backers and investors.

- Compelling Storytelling: Craft a compelling narrative that resonates with your target audience, conveying your passion and purpose.

- Effective Marketing: Leverage digital platforms, social media, and networking to raise awareness about your campaign or venture.

- Transparency and Communication: Foster open and transparent communication with backers, investors, and stakeholders.

Innovative funding models have revolutionized the way entrepreneurs and innovators raise capital for their ventures. From the expansive world of crowdfunding to venture capital, blockchain funding, and beyond, a diverse array of options empowers individuals and organizations to turn their visions into reality. By carefully assessing your needs, aligning with your mission, and leveraging the right funding model, you can embark on a journey of growth, innovation, and impact that transforms your dreams into tangible achievements. Whether you're launching a startup, fueling a creative project, or driving social change, the realm of innovative funding models offers a spectrum of possibilities to shape a brighter future.

CONCLUSION

Embracing Unconventional Paths: Building a Sustainable and Fulfilling Financial Future

In a world of endless possibilities and evolving norms, the conventional path to financial success is no longer the only road worth taking. Embracing unconventional paths has become a powerful way to build a sustainable and fulfilling financial future. This article dives into the concept of charting your own course, exploring alternative routes to financial well-being that prioritize passion, purpose, and creativity.

Redefining Financial Success:

Conventional notions of financial success often revolve around climbing the corporate ladder, amassing wealth, and adhering to predefined societal norms. However, the pursuit of unconventional paths invites a broader perspective—one that values personal growth, meaningful experiences, and a genuine connection to one's work.

The Unconventional Journey:

- Pursuing Passion Projects: Embracing your passions as potential income streams is a hallmark of an unconventional journey. Whether it's turning your hobby into a business or creating content about your interests, passion can fuel both financial success and personal fulfillment.

- Entrepreneurship and Innovation: Entrepreneurial ventures are an unconventional yet impactful way to create value. Innovate, solve problems, and carve out niches that align with your skills and passions.

- Remote Work and Digital Nomadism: Leveraging technology to work remotely or adopt a digital nomad lifestyle allows you to decouple work from location, opening doors to unique experiences and income streams.

- Artistic Pursuits and Creative Expression: For artists, writers, musicians, and creators, unconventional paths can involve pursuing creative endeavors that resonate with audiences while generating income.

- Social Impact and Non-Profit Work: Devoting your career to social impact or non-profit work allows you to blend financial stability with the fulfillment of making a difference.

Crafting Your Unconventional Path:

- Self-Discovery: Reflect on your strengths, interests, and passions. Identify what truly excites you and explore ways to weave those elements into your financial journey.

- Market Research: Research the demand for your skills, services, or products within your chosen unconventional path. Identify gaps and opportunities.

- Continuous Learning: Unconventional paths often require adaptability and continuous learning. Stay curious, open to new experiences, and willing to embrace change.

- Networking and Collaboration: Forge connections with like-minded individuals, mentors, and potential collaborators. Networking can open doors to new opportunities and insights.

Navigating Challenges:

- Risk Management: Unconventional paths may involve more uncertainty. Prioritize risk management, contingency planning, and building a safety net.

- Mindset Shift: Challenge societal norms and redefine your perception of success. Focus on intrinsic motivation and the impact you're making.

- Financial Literacy: Acquire financial literacy skills to manage income, expenses, investments, and savings effectively.

- Resilience: Embrace setbacks as learning experiences and cultivate resilience to overcome challenges.

Balancing Passion and Pragmatism:

While passion is a powerful driving force, pragmatic considerations are equally important. Striking a balance between what you love and what provides financial stability ensures a sustainable journey.

Embracing unconventional paths represents a departure from the traditional route to financial success, enabling individuals to forge unique and deeply meaningful journeys. By weaving passion, purpose, and creativity into their financial pursuits, people can create a tapestry of experiences that enrich their lives and the lives of others. Whether you're an artist, an entrepreneur, a social advocate, or someone exploring the uncharted territories of your interests, the world of unconventional paths offers a canvas where you can paint your own definition of success, fulfillment, and financial well-being.

Appendix

Resources and Tools: A Comprehensive Guide for Aspiring Unconventional Entrepreneurs

Embarking on an unconventional entrepreneurial journey requires a unique blend of creativity, resilience, and strategic thinking. To help aspiring unconventional entrepreneurs navigate this path, here's a comprehensive guide featuring essential resources and tools to support your endeavors and bring your innovative ideas to life.

1. Self-Discovery and Idea Generation:

The Ikigai Diagram: Explore the intersection of what you love, what you're good at, what the world needs, and what you can be paid for. This can help you uncover your true passion and purpose.

Mind Mapping Tools: Use tools like MindMeister or XMind to visually brainstorm and organize your ideas, helping you clarify your vision and potential business concepts.

2. Market Research and Validation:

Google Trends: Analyze search trends to gauge the popularity and demand for your chosen niche or idea.

SurveyMonkey or Typeform: Create surveys to gather insights from potential customers and validate your concept before diving in.

Social Media Listening Tools: Tools like Hootsuite or Brandwatch allow you to monitor social media conversations to identify trends and customer needs.

3. Business Planning and Strategy:

Business Model Canvas: Create a visual representation of your business model, highlighting key components such as value proposition, customer segments, revenue streams, and more.

Lean Startup Methodology: Follow the principles of the Lean Startup approach to build a minimum viable product (MVP) and iterate based on user feedback.

4. Funding and Financing:

Kickstarter or Indiegogo: Launch crowdfunding campaigns to secure initial funding and test the market demand for your product or service.

AngelList: Connect with angel investors who are interested in supporting innovative startups.

Grants and Competitions: Explore opportunities for grants and business competitions that align with your unconventional venture.

5. Building Your Online Presence:

Website Builders: Platforms like WordPress, Wix, or Squarespace enable you to create a professional website to showcase your offerings.

Social Media Platforms: Utilize platforms like Instagram, Twitter, Facebook, and LinkedIn to connect with your target audience and share your journey.

Content Creation Tools: Tools like Canva or Adobe Spark help you design eye-catching visuals and graphics for your online presence.

6. Remote Work and Collaboration:

Remote Collaboration Tools: Use tools like Slack, Microsoft Teams, or Trello to communicate and collaborate with your team, regardless of geographical location.

Video Conferencing: Platforms like Zoom or Google Meet facilitate virtual meetings and presentations.

7. Financial Management:

Accounting Software: Tools like QuickBooks or FreshBooks help you manage your finances, track expenses, and generate invoices.

Budgeting Apps: Use apps like Mint or YNAB to create and stick to a budget, helping you maintain financial stability.

8. Learning and Skill Development:

Online Learning Platforms: Platforms like Coursera, Udemy, and Skillshare offer courses to enhance your skills in areas such as entrepreneurship, marketing, design, and more.

Books and Podcasts: Explore a wealth of entrepreneurial wisdom and insights from books and podcasts dedicated to unconventional entrepreneurship.

9. Networking and Mentorship:

Meetup: Find local or virtual meetups and networking events relevant to your industry or interests.

LinkedIn: Connect with fellow entrepreneurs, mentors, and potential collaborators on this professional networking platform.

10. Mental Health and Well-Being:

Meditation Apps: Use apps like Headspace or Calm to incorporate mindfulness and stress relief into your routine.

Supportive Communities: Join online communities or forums where unconventional entrepreneurs share experiences, challenges, and advice.

Embarking on an unconventional entrepreneurial journey is an exciting and transformative endeavor. By leveraging these resources and tools, you can navigate the challenges and uncertainties with confidence, harness your creativity, and craft a path that not only aligns with your passions but also brings meaningful impact to your life and the lives of others. Remember, the road less traveled may be unconventional, but it holds boundless potential for innovation, growth, and fulfillment.